To Brian,
   Hope you are able to visit this fine Museum one day.
      Love,
      Cliff & Judy Abrams.

1998
Royal Tyrrel Museum of Palaeontology
Drumheller, Alberta
Canada.

GRAVEYARDS OF THE DINOSAURS

First published in Canada in 1998 by
Scholastic Canada Ltd.
123 Newkirk Road
Richmond Hill, Ontario L4C 3G5

Canadian Cataloguing in Publication Data
Tanaka, Shelley
Graveyards of the dinosaurs : what it is like to discover prehistoric creatures

(I was there)
ISBN 0-590-12446-3 (bound) ISBN 0-590-12447-1 (pbk.)

1. Dinosaurs — Juvenile literature. 2. Paleontology — Juvenile literature. I. Title. II. Series.

QE862.D5T36 1998   J567.9   C97-931933-1

Design and Art Direction: Gordon Sibley Design Inc.
Illustrations: Alan Barnard, Mark Hallett, John Sibbick, Michael Skrepnick
Diagrams and Maps: Jack McMaster
Editorial Director: Hugh M. Brewster
Project Editor: Nan Froman
Editorial Assistance: Susan Aihoshi
Production Director: Susan Barrable
Production Co-ordinator: Donna Chong
Color Separation: Colour Technologies
Printing and Binding: Artegrafica S.p.A.

Graveyards of the Dinosaurs was produced by Madison Press Books,
which is under the direction of Albert E. Cummings.

Madison Press Books
40 Madison Avenue
Toronto, Ontario
Canada M5R 2S1

Endpapers: The badlands of Dinosaur Provincial Park, Alberta.
Previous page: Fossils of an *Oviraptor* and its egg.
Right: A *T. rex* is startled by the sight of a giant asteriod hurtling toward the earth.
Overleaf: A *Velociraptor* skull found in the Gobi Desert. (Left inset) An *Oviraptor* on its nest.
(Middle inset) Paleontologist Phil Currie at work.
(Right inset) The huge skull of *Carcharodontosaurus* compared to a human skull.

Printed in Italy

GRAVEYARDS OF THE DINOSAURS

What it's like to discover prehistoric creatures

BY SHELLEY TANAKA

Paleontological consultation by
Philip J. Currie, Mark Norell, and Paul Sereno

Featuring illustrations by Alan Barnard

A SCHOLASTIC/MADISON PRESS BOOK

Contents

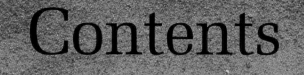

Prologue

Far away, in the heart of the earth's largest continent, stretches a vast desert — the Gobi.
It is as barren and as unwelcoming as the moon. During the long winters the ragged valleys and
plains are covered with snow and swept by icy gales. In the summer blistering heat
oozes out of the hot sand and gravel. From time to time, choking sandstorms gallop in like furies.
The fierce wind blasts away at the rocks and sweeps sand off the red cliffs. And sometimes
it reveals ancient remains that have lain undisturbed for millions of years....

More than seventy years ago, an American explorer named Roy Chapman Andrews traveled halfway around the world to uncover some of the Gobi's secrets. He was not a typical scientist. When he was a boy growing up in Wisconsin, school was sheer torture. He couldn't wait for the bell to ring every afternoon so he could ramble through the fields and canoe the rivers near his home. He caught frogs and salamanders. He tramped through the marshes, hunting wild ducks with his trusty single-barreled shotgun.

There was nothing Roy loved better than looking for creatures and exploring nature's wild places. As a young man he got a job at the American Museum of

Near the Flaming Cliffs in the Gobi Desert of Mongolia (above), many dinosaur bones have been found including those of the fierce Velociraptor *(far left).*

Natural History, in New York, sweeping floors and scrubbing display tables just to get his foot in the door. He stuffed hundreds of dead animals for display. One winter he even scraped rotting flesh off a beached whale so the museum could display the skeleton.

His hard work paid off. In 1922, he led an expedition to the Gobi to look for ancient fossils. It was the largest scientific land expedition ever launched.

Everyone said it was a crazy idea, and it is true that the Central Asiatic Expedition was quite a sight.

7

Roy Chapman Andrews (pictured at left of inset) led several scientific expeditions to the Gobi Desert. A procession of camels was often used to carry heavy equipment through the sand dunes.

A caravan of seventy-five bad-tempered camels paraded slowly across the desert. The animals grunted and complained as hundreds of pounds of spare tires, tents, food, photographic equipment, and gasoline barrels slapped against their flanks. Later came the motorcars with the Americans in their neatly pressed khaki outfits, their pipe smoke mingling with the smells of the camels.

From time to time Roy Chapman Andrews would race his car against a thundering herd of wild asses, honking his horn like a maniac. He loved to stand up and aim his rifle over the hood of the car, warning off parties of bandits or trying to shoot an antelope for dinner.

It may have seemed like fun, but the goal of the expedition was deadly serious. Roy Chapman Andrews and his team were looking for ancient remains to prove that Asia was the birthplace of all human and animal life.

They never found what they were looking for. Instead, they uncovered something far more interesting.

Less than one week into the expedition, on a ledge near the camp, the team found a large leg bone outlined against the surrounding rock.

It belonged to a dinosaur.

Roy Chapman Andrews didn't know it yet, but he had just discovered one of the richest dinosaur graveyards in the world.

The Central Asiatic Expedition returned to America with fourteen dinosaur skeletons and seventy skulls belonging to *Protoceratops* (an uncle of *Triceratops* and *Centrosaurus*), *Oviraptor*, and the fast-running killer, *Velociraptor*. They also returned with the first dinosaur eggs known to science.

Their discoveries would change the way the world looked at these strange beasts. What were the dinosaurs really like? Were they just ugly, dumb reptiles, chomping their way through prehistoric swamps? Why were they able to survive for an astonishing 165 million years, becoming, in some cases, the biggest, fiercest creatures the world has ever known? And what could they tell us about life on our planet today?

In the Gobi, Roy Chapman Andrews made one of the most remarkable scientific discoveries of the century. His story inspired many young paleontologists to continue his adventure. In time, they would discover some remarkable things not only about how dinosaurs died, but about how they lived.

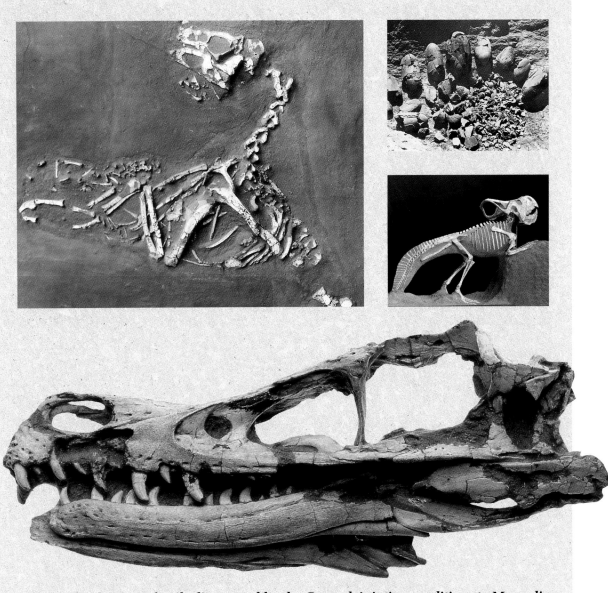

Among the dinosaur fossils discovered by the Central Asiatic expeditions to Mongolia were an Oviraptor *skeleton (top left), a nest containing dinosaur eggs (top right), and a complete skeleton of* Protoceratops *(bottom right). They also found skulls belonging to* Velociraptors *(above).*

Part I
The Gobi Desert
Mongolia

Seventy years after Roy Chapman Andrews made his famous discoveries, the American Museum of Natural History sent another expedition to Mongolia. This time, there was no long camel caravan. The team, led by paleontologists Michael Novacek and Mark Norell, traveled with an old Russian military truck, a gasoline tanker, and a few four-wheel-drive vehicles. The scientists sported sunglasses, baseball caps, ragged shorts, and beards, instead of high leather boots, wide-brimmed hats, and trim khaki outfits. Instead of shooting antelopes for dinner, they ate freeze-dried pork chops.

The desert, on the other hand, hadn't changed. In the terrible heat of high afternoon, their tents would be too hot to touch. There were still hardly any real roads, and the ones that were available were poorly mapped and sometimes thickly covered with sand. On a bad day it could take seven hours to travel thirty miles (forty-eight kilometers). The flies settled around their ears like clouds, scorpions hid under sleeping bags, and the desert sand was everywhere — in their hair, their eyes, even in their underwear.

But the scientists didn't care, because the Gobi was still one of the best dinosaur graveyards in the world.

When he was seven, Michael Novacek had loved Roy Chapman Andrews's children's book, *All About Dinosaurs*. He had got into trouble for poring over the drawings of Andrews's camel caravan instead of paying attention in class. Now he and Norell were retracing the steps of his childhood hero.

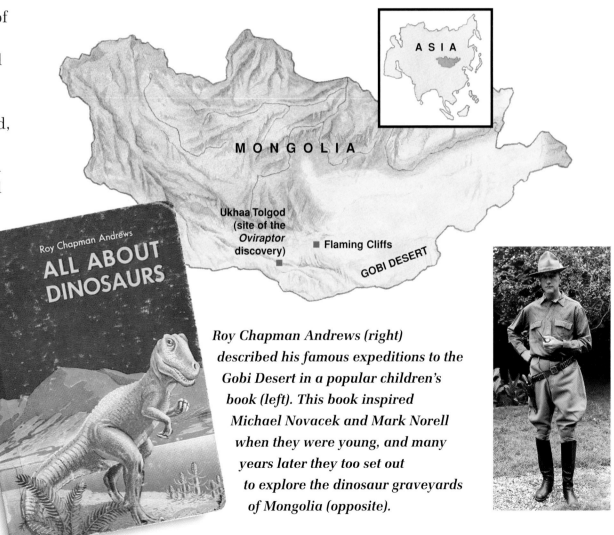

Roy Chapman Andrews (right) described his famous expeditions to the Gobi Desert in a popular children's book (left). This book inspired Michael Novacek and Mark Norell when they were young, and many years later they too set out to explore the dinosaur graveyards of Mongolia (opposite).

11

One of the Central Asiatic Expedition's most amazing accomplishments was finding proof that dinosaurs laid eggs. The team had found nests full of them. The eggs looked like big baked potatoes with wrinkled

Paleontologist Mark Norell gently scrapes earth away from a nest of dinosaur eggs.

skins. They lay in tidy circles. Nearby, the paleontologists also found many skeletons and skulls belonging to *Protoceratops*, a sheep-sized, plant-eating dinosaur.

Then they came across a different creature lying on top of one of the nests. This skeleton belonged to a parrot-faced, meat-eating dinosaur.

Andrews and his team imagined the scene. The eggs, they figured, lay in a *Protoceratops* nest. The parrot-headed carnivore must have died while trying to steal the eggs. It could have crushed those shells in an instant with its powerful beak, so it could suck up the contents.

They called the carnivore *Oviraptor*, the egg thief.

Now Novacek and Norell were back near Andrews's territory, wandering over the red sand, searching for signs of white bone. Like Andrews, they found plenty of fossils belonging to *Protoceratops*. They also found nests full of eggs that looked exactly like the ones Andrews had found. On top of one of the nests lay the child-sized skeleton of *Oviraptor*, caught in the act of egg-stealing, according to Roy Chapman Andrews's scenario.

Then, some distance from the *Oviraptor*-covered nest, Mark Norell discovered several other nests filled with eggs similar to the ones they had already found. And curled inside one of the eggs was a tiny skeleton belonging to an unhatched baby *Oviraptor*.

The *Oviraptor* lying on top of the nest wasn't stealing *Protoceratops* eggs at all. It was sitting on a nest containing its own eggs. The texture of the rock in which the fossils were found suggested that the dinosaur had been buried, perhaps by a sandstorm or a collapsing sand dune.

What happened to the *Oviraptor*?

Scientists made a rare find in the Gobi Desert: the skeleton of an *Oviraptor* on top of a nest of eggs. The birdlike dinosaur may have been buried by a sandstorm or by a collapsing sand dune following heavy rains. Here is what happened from the time of the *Oviraptor*'s death, about seventy million years ago, until its discovery.

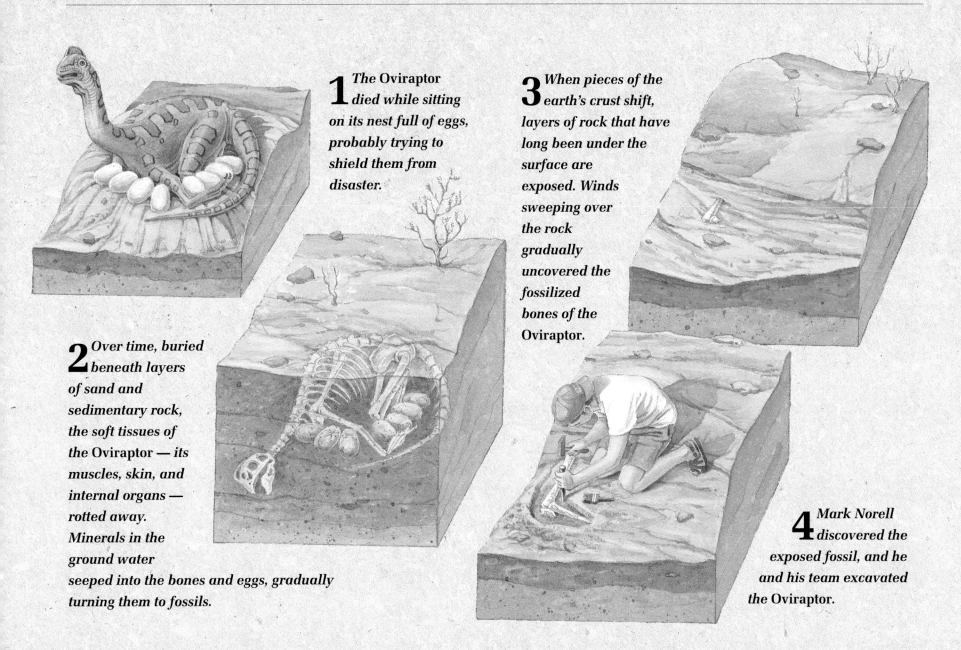

1 The Oviraptor died while sitting on its nest full of eggs, probably trying to shield them from disaster.

2 Over time, buried beneath layers of sand and sedimentary rock, the soft tissues of the Oviraptor — *its muscles, skin, and internal organs* — *rotted away. Minerals in the ground water seeped into the bones and eggs, gradually turning them to fossils.*

3 When pieces of the earth's crust shift, layers of rock that have long been under the surface are exposed. Winds sweeping over the rock gradually uncovered the fossilized bones of the Oviraptor.

4 Mark Norell discovered the exposed fossil, and he and his team excavated the Oviraptor.

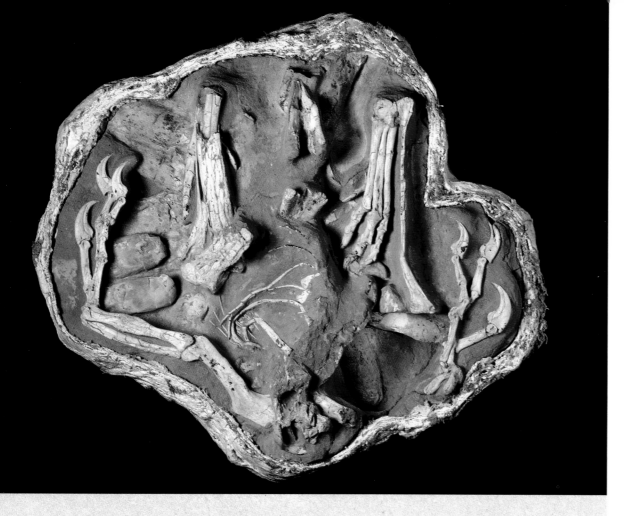

Oviraptor was not an egg thief, as Andrews's team had thought. Instead, it appeared to have been a devoted parent who died while protecting its eggs. It had built a nest and carefully laid its eggs in a circle. After the eggs had hatched, it may have cared for the hatchlings, feeding them and shielding them from harm.

Seventy million years ago, the Gobi Desert was sprinkled with lakes that overflowed during the wet season and dried up during the hottest months. These areas drew creatures of all kinds and provided good hunting territory for predators.

(Right)
Oviraptor
shelters its young from a fierce desert sandstorm.

Two small skulls belonging to a meat-eating dinosaur were also found in the nest containing the unhatched egg. What were they doing there? We will never know for sure, but most likely they were killed and brought to the nest by the adult *Oviraptor*, as food for its own babies.

The idea that dinosaurs looked after their young is a fairly new one. For a long time they were thought to have simply laid their

"Big Mama" *Oviraptor*

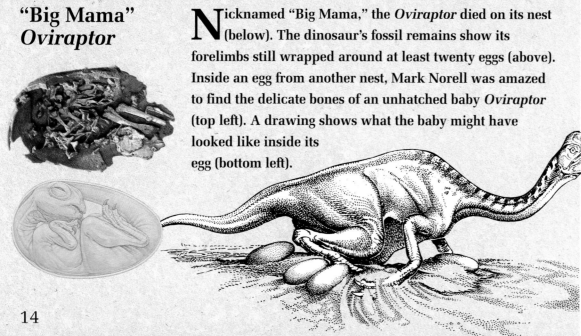

Nicknamed "Big Mama," the *Oviraptor* died on its nest (below). The dinosaur's fossil remains show its forelimbs still wrapped around at least twenty eggs (above). Inside an egg from another nest, Mark Norell was amazed to find the delicate bones of an unhatched baby *Oviraptor* (top left). A drawing shows what the baby might have looked like inside its egg (bottom left).

The Battling Dinosaurs

An amazing fossil find excavated in Mongolia, in 1971, revealed the complete skeletons of a *Velociraptor* and a *Protoceratops* caught in a deadly fight before being buried in a sandstorm. The *Velociraptor*'s hand was found clutching the frill of the *Protoceratops*, while its sickle-shaped slashing foot claw was embedded in the body of its enemy. The *Protoceratops* attempted to defend itself by biting the arm of the *Velociraptor*.

eggs and left the young to hatch and fend for themselves, just like other modern reptiles. Instead, *Oviraptor* seemed to behave very much like a bird.

Paleontologists know that there is a limit to what bones can reveal about dinosaurs. Bones can tell us what kind of dinosaurs we are looking at and their overall size and shape. Teeth and claws may give us clues about what kind of food they ate and how they caught it.

But bones, teeth, and claws cannot tell us everything about how dinosaurs behaved. A sharp, curved claw may have been used as a weapon, but it may also have been used to dig for insects or build nests. A skeleton of a baby meat-eater found in an *Oviraptor* nest may have been put there for free baby-sitting, the way cuckoos place their eggs in other birds' nests today. It may have been food for the adult *Oviraptor*. Or it may have been brought to the nest as food for the hatchlings.

Today's paleontologists want to do more than collect and identify bones. It makes sense to draw on our whole range of scientific knowledge to help us understand dinosaurs. We can look at similarities between dinosaurs and living creatures. We can use computers to track individual physical traits through millions of years of evolution to see how different creatures may be related to each other.

For some time, scientists have suspected that there is a strong link between birds and carnivorous dinosaurs like *Oviraptor*. They share more than 125 unique skeletal features. Both have inner toes that

Are birds living dinosaurs?

Fossil evidence shows that birds and some carnivorous dinosaurs are likely closely related. The remains of the earliest known bird, *Archaeopteryx* (above), shared some characteristics with dinosaurs such as claws, teeth, and a long bony tail, although it also had feathers. And there is a striking resemblance between the skeletons of *Struthiomimus*, a dinosaur that lived seventy million years ago, and an ostrich. Both animals have long, curving necks, long legs, and toothless beaks.

Struthiomimus

Ostrich

Good Mother Lizard

In 1978 paleontologist Jack Horner went to a rock shop in northern Montana where he saw tiny bones that he immediately recognized as the fossils of baby duckbill dinosaurs. He began to dig where the bones had been found and soon uncovered a giant nest made of mud, 6 feet (2 m) in diameter and 3 feet (1 m) deep. It contained the bones of baby dinosaurs and crushed eggshells, indicating that the babies had stayed in the nest after hatching, stepping on shells over and over again. Horner concluded that the babies had been fed in the nest (above), just as many young birds are nurtured by their parents. Until this discovery, it was assumed that dinosaurs simply let their young fend for themselves, the way most modern reptiles do.

Horner and his team eventually found dozens of nests arranged in a tightly packed colony. He named the duckbill dinosaur *Maiasaura*, Greek for "good mother lizard."

point backward. Both walk on two legs and have long arms. They have similar hollow bones, eye structures, and brain shapes. The skulls of a *Velociraptor* and an ostrich, for example, are almost identical in some parts. Both lay hard eggs with similar eggshell. And dinosaurs like *Oviraptor*s have wishbones, just like birds.

So are birds descended from dinosaurs? Are birds a kind of dinosaur, just as humans are a kind of mammal?

Most paleontologists now think so. Many even think some dinosaurs may have had feathers.

Does this mean that dinosaurs shared many behaviors with modern birds? Did they care for their young, gather in flocks, teach their babies how to find food and survive outside the nest? Did they migrate? Were dinosaurs as clever as crows, or as stupid as farmyard turkeys?

The *Oviraptor* graveyard that Novacek and Norell found raised many new questions about dinosaur behavior. Indeed, scientists are realizing that dinosaurs may have been far more complicated creatures than they had ever imagined.

Baby Dinosaurs

Some experts think that baby dinosaurs were as appealing as puppies, with big heads, fat bodies, and long legs. If so, their cuddly appearance may have stimulated their parents to look after them. Baby snakes are born looking much as they will when they are adults, and they are left to care for themselves.

The valley was quiet. *Oviraptor* peered into her nest. She had made it carefully, choosing a spot partway up the slope. That way her eggs wouldn't be drowned when the pond flooded during the wet season. She had laid her eggs two at a time, turning in the nest to create a tidy spiral as she scooped sand onto each newly laid pair. Then she had sat on them patiently until they were ready to hatch.

Some of the babies had already pushed their way out of their shells. Dark cracks streaked the surface of many of the remaining eggs.

The cries of the hungry hatchlings grew louder as they blindly nipped at the air with their tiny beaks. They had already picked clean the bones of two young meat-eaters that she had brought to the nest the day before.

Oviraptor raised her head and sniffed the air. Normally she would wait for twilight to hunt, but she was hungry, too.

She trotted down the hill toward the pond. The sand was littered with the tracks of creatures that regularly came to the oasis to drink. In the shallows a crocodile slipped its head back into the water as she approached.

She scanned a small overhang at the edge of a sandy outcropping. Then her large eyes caught movement. A small lizard slithered out from under a rock. In seconds she snatched it up and crushed its body with her strong beak before swallowing it whole.

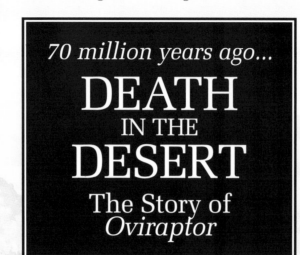

70 million years ago...

DEATH
IN THE
DESERT
The Story of *Oviraptor*

There was a stirring in a patch of prickly bushes. A small, furry creature with a long tail poked its nose out of the branches right in front of her. She was about to grab it when her attention was caught by something bigger. Two large shadows loomed up from the other side of the brush.

The *Velociraptors* leaped toward her at the same time, their teeth bared. They were smaller than she was, but they were very fast. Their sickle claws could rip open flesh with a single slash.

Oviraptor rose up and leaned back on her tail. She opened her beak in a sharp cry. Her head crest sliced the sky and cast a long shadow over her attackers. She spread her big-clawed fingers and lashed out with powerful arms.

The *Velociraptors* leaped back and moved apart until she could no longer see both of them at once. Her head moved back and forth between them.

They all heard the storm before they saw it. It came roaring across the desert, a swirling, shrieking cyclone of sand. The sky grew dark as the hot, choking wall blew in. The *Velociraptors* vanished.

Oviraptor raced back to her nest, screaming as grains of sand stung her on all sides. Sand filled her mouth and eyes. She stumbled blindly into the nest, crushing two of her eggs. She crouched over the others, tucking her legs beneath her body. She dug her toes into the sand and curled her arms around her babies.

Then everything was lost in the roar of the storm.

Part II
Dinosaur Provincial Park
Alberta, Canada

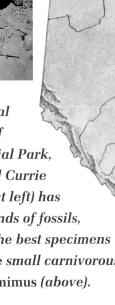

Among the unusual rock formations of Dinosaur Provincial Park, Alberta (left), Phil Currie (pictured above, at left) has excavated thousands of fossils, including one of the best specimens in the world of the small carnivorous dinosaur Ornithomimus *(above).*

ALBERTA

CANADA
U.S.A.

Dinosaur
Provincial
Park

Unhappily for paleontologists, the best dinosaur graveyards are often found in the most bleak, lonely areas on earth. But these empty places also have a mysterious and awesome beauty. You can feel as if you have just landed on the planet for the first time.

Dinosaur Provincial Park, in southern Alberta, is such a place. It's cowboy country. The land is dotted with cactus and sagebrush. Golden eagles and falcons nest on the cliffs. Rock columns rise out of the valleys like chubby-stemmed mushrooms, casting eerie shadows.

The park is also loaded with dinosaur bones. They roll out of the hillsides as the rain and wind whisk sandstone off the cliff walls and valley floor. More kinds of dinosaurs have been found here than anywhere else on earth.

Phil Currie is head of dinosaur research at the Royal Tyrrell Museum of Palaeontology. Located near the park, it is one of the largest dinosaur museums in the world.

Currie has found many dinosaur fossils. He knows what it is like to come across a bone sticking out of the earth, then brush away the sand until a complete skeleton lies uncovered. He says that removing that final layer of sand is like unveiling a work of art. You can look at the skeleton and imagine the powerful muscles, tough skin, and fierce expression that once went with the bones.

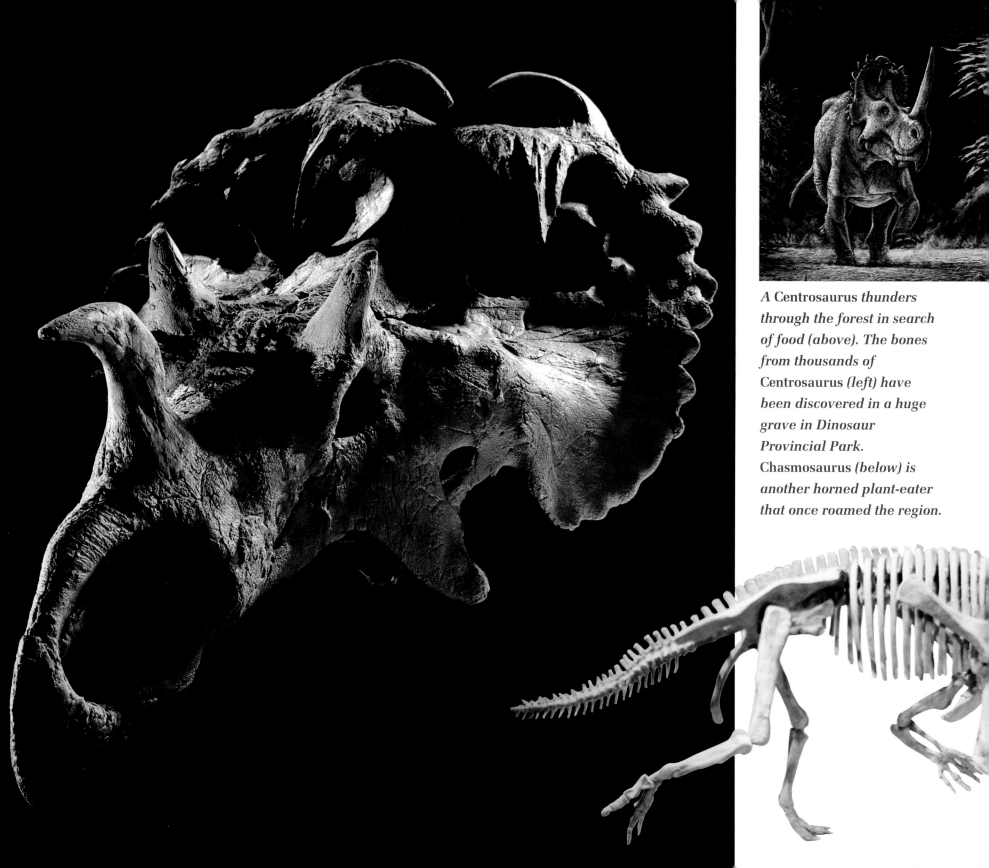

A Centrosaurus *thunders through the forest in search of food (above). The bones from thousands of* Centrosaurus *(left) have been discovered in a huge grave in Dinosaur Provincial Park.* Chasmosaurus *(below) is another horned plant-eater that once roamed the region.*

Currie has loved dinosaurs ever since he pulled a plastic figurine out of a cereal box when he was six years old. As a boy, he would fish chicken bones out of the kitchen garbage and wrap them in plaster and burlap to practice his excavation techniques. He started a collection of plastic dinosaurs (which he still has today) and built landscapes for them in his basement — complete with a working volcano! And he read *All About Dinosaurs*, the book written by his hero, Roy Chapman Andrews. (In 1988, when Currie was searching for fossils in the Gobi Desert, one of his team's most exciting finds was not a dinosaur but a battered tin flask that Roy Chapman Andrews had taken on one of his famous expeditions.)

Today, Phil Currie is one of the few people who can identify any known carnivorous dinosaur just by looking at a single tooth.

Dinosaur fossils are so common in Dinosaur Provincial Park that finding one is not an earth-shattering event. It is said that if you throw your hat and it doesn't come within twenty feet (six meters) of a dinosaur bone, then you're not in Dinosaur Park. So Currie was not overly excited when a new bed of dinosaur bones was discovered here in 1978. The loose bones seemed to be scattered over an area larger than a football field. There were between twenty to sixty bones per square yard (meter), and it was difficult to walk without stepping on one.

The bones were excavated and examined more closely. And Currie found that most of them belonged to one kind of dinosaur — the horned plant-eater called *Centrosaurus.* The bone bed turned out to be a mass

The Paleontologist's Art

Once a fossil has been discovered, it is photographed, cleaned with a soft brush, and painted with a thin layer of glue so that it won't disintegrate during excavation. Then the surrounding rock is carefully chipped away (top right). A fossil is often so delicate that it cannot be removed unless it is strengthened by wrapping it in plaster and burlap strips, forming a cast (middle right). After the plaster dries, the specimen can be removed from the site. In a museum or laboratory, fossil "preparators" carefully remove the plaster cast and the remaining rock around the fossil, often using fine dental tools. Cleaning, studying, and preparing a large skeleton for display can take years (bottom right).

graveyard containing the remains of thousands of *Centrosaurus* of all ages. All of them, it seemed, had perished in a single overwhelming disaster.

Why had so many *Centrosaurus* gathered in one spot, and how had they died so suddenly?

Millions of years ago, North America was divided by a great inland sea fed by rivers that ran down from highlands where the Rocky Mountains now stand. Fossil remains and ancient dinosaur tracks have shown that the west coast of this sea was a vast migration route. Dinosaurs would travel from breeding sites in the

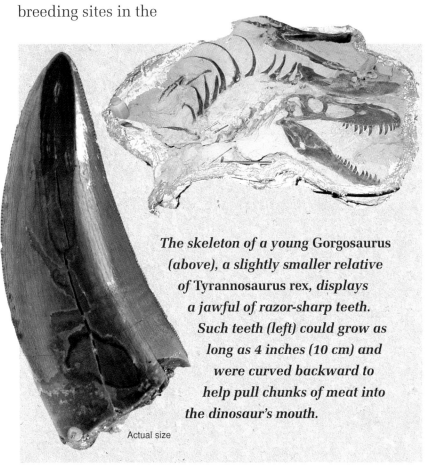

The skeleton of a young Gorgosaurus *(above), a slightly smaller relative of* Tyrannosaurus rex, *displays a jawful of razor-sharp teeth. Such teeth (left) could grow as long as 4 inches (10 cm) and were curved backward to help pull chunks of meat into the dinosaur's mouth.*

Actual size

south to feeding grounds in the north. The land beside the water was lush with flowering magnolias, towering redwoods, and marsh plants. The wetlands were bursting with dragonflies and other insects, frogs, turtles, birds, crocodiles, and small mammals, as well as the larger animals that stopped to drink and feed.

Because their route followed the shoreline, the migrating dinosaurs would have had to cross the rivers that ran into the sea. These crossings usually went smoothly. But a panic in any tightly packed crowd can end suddenly and tragically. Caribou herds have died in this way during river crossings.

(Right) Until recently the fearsome hunter Gorgosaurus *was thought to be the same dinosaur as* Albertosaurus.

Phil Currie found that many of the *Centrosaurus* bones had marks showing that they were broken just after death, suggesting that the bodies may have been trampled. They would have washed up on the shore, where they were eaten by scavengers. Some bones had teeth marks, and the serrated teeth of carnivores, including those of *Gorgosaurus*, were found among the bones. Meat-eating dinosaurs routinely lost and replaced teeth. They had likely fed on the bodies, their loose teeth falling out as they tore at the flesh and skin.

Once the flesh had been eaten or rotted away from the *Centrosaurus* bones, the skeletons would have fallen apart and been mixed up by the river. Eventually they were covered by sand washed down from the uplands.

The idea that dinosaurs traveled in herds raises many questions for paleontologists, particularly when they look at the fancy headgear of *Centrosaurus*. The nose horns are easy to explain. They could have been formidable

weapons, capable of piercing the belly of a deadly tyrannosaur like *Gorgosaurus.*

But what about the neck frills? Some had hooks curved forward like can openers. Others were curved back like coat hooks.

Were they used by males to attract females and assert their position in the herd, the way many antlered animals do today? Did they use their horns to wrestle with each other for mates or territory? Horned dinosaurs have been found with punctures in their cheeks and frills, suggesting to some that the animals did fight amongst themselves.

And how did these herds come together? Did they gather at nesting sites and use the same routes every year? Fossils of Alberta dinosaurs have been found in the Canadian Arctic, where the summer days are long and the vegetation is thick and lush for a few months a year. Ancient trackways containing thousands of footprints of plant-eating dinosaurs have been discovered running

swiftly as they chased their prey. Scientists can also gauge speed from these tracks. They know, for example, that some meat-eating dinosaurs could run between 28 and 30 miles per hour (45 and 50 kph). They can sometimes even tell whether individual dinosaurs were babies or adults. About 1,700 dinosaur footprints have been found in the canyon of the Peace River in British Columbia, Canada (left).

Dinosaur Footprints

By studying dinosaur tracks left along the shores of ancient lakes and rivers, paleontologists can tell whether they were left by plant-eaters, browsing as they moved in herds, or by meat-eaters, running

along the eastern edge of the Rocky Mountains.

Did the dinosaurs spread out once they reached their feeding grounds, then gather together again before returning south? How fast would a herd of dinosaurs have to move to cover such a long distance, while eating huge amounts of vegetation along the way just to keep themselves going? Did they care for the young ones as they traveled, perhaps keeping them in the center of the herd the way musk ox and buffalo do today?

Horns and Frills

These dinosaurs, which are from the same family as *Centrosaurus*, sported a great variety of nose horns, eyebrow horns, and head frills. The delicate spikes around the frill of *Styracosaurus* were most likely used for display, but its long nose horn could have been a deadly weapon.

Did parents recognize their own young and look after them? Did the herd share its food resources, or was it every *Centrosaurus* for itself? And what happened to the forests and parklands that they passed through, eating and trampling everything in sight?

The *Centrosaurus* bone bed kept Phil Currie and his team busy for two decades. The more they found out, the more questions they raised about how dinosaurs lived together.

Triceratops had sturdy long eyebrow horns which it probably used to defend itself.

Pachyrhinosaurus, one of the largest horned dinosaurs, had an unusual round bone on its snout instead of a horn. These spectacular animals were the last major group of dinosaurs to evolve.

Pachyrhinosaurus

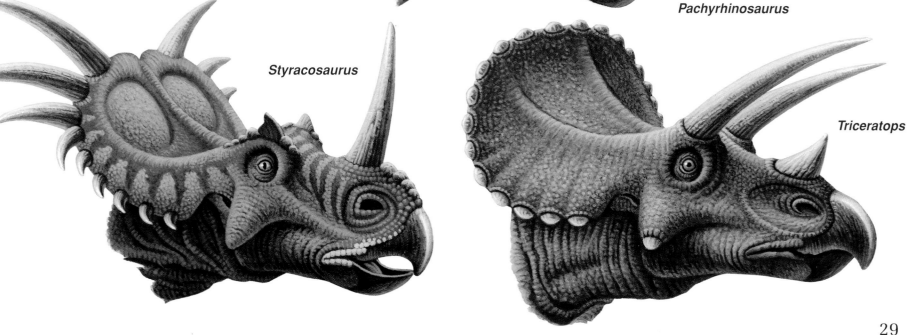

Styracosaurus

Triceratops

29

The ground trembled with the sound of beasts. Hundreds of *Centrosaurus* lumbered down to the muddy river shore. They tore at the magnolias and trampled the young pines that lined the stream bed. They walked and ate, sometimes knocking over small trees with their heads before stripping off the leaves and twigs. They ripped at the bushes and ferns, leaving a wasteland of stumps and broken branches behind them.

The clouds hung low over the valley. There had been several days of heavy rainfall and another storm was coming. The moist air was thick with the smell of dung and decaying plants.

75 million years ago...
A FATAL RIVER CROSSING
The Story of *Centrosaurus*

In the shadows of a redwood grove near the edge of the clearing, *Gorgosaurus* waited. This was good hunting territory. *Centrosaurus* herds came this way every year, and there were always plenty of young ones.

As the herd pushed toward the water, one of the young beasts straggled behind, stopping to wallow in the cooling mud. It bleated as it tried to catch up to the rest of the herd. Its neck frill was short and undeveloped. Its hornless snout looked soft and naked.

Gorgosaurus dashed out from the forest with a bellow, its powerful hind legs pumping and its tail held high. The noise caught the attention of two males at the

rear of the herd. They turned quickly, pointing their vicious horns toward the attacker. The young one hurried into the center of the herd, while the males made short, thrusting steps toward the enemy.

Gorgosaurus stopped and reared. Then it pulled back into the trees. There would be no meal this time.

The herd had been disturbed by the commotion. As the leader waded into the rising river to cross, the others pressed in too close behind. The peaceful crossing was suddenly thrown into confusion.

Two huge males shoved against each other and turned to lock horns.

Then, above the noise of the herd, thunder cracked over the hills to the west. The water churned with the baying and crashing of the beasts, as more and more animals stumbled into the water. They pushed each other under, scrabbling for a foothold on the drowning bodies in front. The young were quickly trampled into the mud.

As the panic rose, some turned around and tried to make their way back to the shore. Overhead, birds screamed.

When it was all over, bodies littered the shoreline and floated in the river. As the days passed, bloated carcasses drifted downstream and became caught on sandbars and in fallen trees.

The stink of rotting bodies quickly penetrated the surrounding forest. *Gorgosaurus* followed the scent to the river, where the noise of the flies was almost deafening. Birds, pterosaurs, crocodiles, and other scavengers were already picking at the carcasses. They didn't even scatter at the approach of the beast.

There was plenty of meat here for everyone.

Part III

Valley of the Moon

Argentina

The Valley of the Moon is well named. It is a rugged, empty desert surrounded by towering cliffs. The snow-capped peaks of the Andes Mountains loom in the distance. But at the beginning of the dinosaur age, this was a lush river valley crawling with life. It is one of the oldest dinosaur graveyards in the world — one of the few places where you can find fossils that are more than 220 million years old.

In 1988, Paul Sereno set out on a six-week expedition to uncover some of these fossils.

Like Roy Chapman Andrews, Paul Sereno wasn't wild about school when he was a boy. "I wasn't reading in second grade," he says. "I couldn't tell time in third grade, and I nearly flunked sixth grade." He was very good at getting into trouble, however, whether he was falling off his bike, throwing rocks at the school windows, or tossing apples into the band players' tubas.

Then came the crime that turned his life around. He stole a book from the school library. It was a book about fossils.

Sereno is now a university professor and one of the most respected dinosaur experts in the world. He has retraced the steps of Roy Chapman Andrews, searching for dinosaurs in the Gobi. He has also found one of the world's biggest carnivores, *Carcharodontosaurus*, in North Africa.

Paul Sereno (opposite) has led several expeditions to the Valley of the Moon, Argentina (above), one of the only places on earth where fossils from the very earliest dinosaurs have been found.

But one of Sereno's most dramatic discoveries came near the beginning of his career, when he set out to chart the entire evolution of dinosaurs. To do this, he had to start with the earliest dinosaur yet known — *Herrerasaurus*. Although a number of *Herrerasaurus* fossils had been found, there weren't enough bones to tell him exactly what the creature had looked like. Most important, no one had ever discovered a complete skull.

33

Sereno decided to look for a complete skeleton himself. That is how he ended up in the Valley of the Moon, the place where the other *Herrerasaurus* fossils had been found.

And just how was he going to find this rare skeleton? As Phil Currie has said, finding fossils is painfully simple. You walk, and you look.

It was like looking for a needle in a haystack.

S ereno and his team were combing the area piece by piece, gradually making their way along the valley. As they drove away from one spot, he realized there

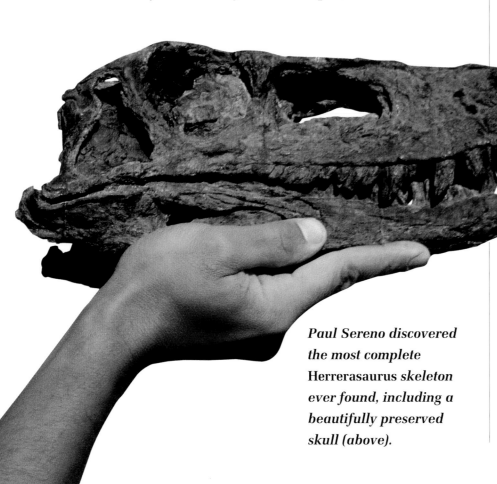

Paul Sereno discovered the most complete Herrerasaurus **skeleton ever found, including a beautifully preserved skull (above).**

was a small ravine that they had missed. They moved on anyway, but that small triangle of land nagged at him. He couldn't sleep. So, a few weeks later, they drove back to it.

Most paleontologists will tell you that there are some field workers who have a special knack for finding fossils. Some call it accident or luck. Some say it's a sixth sense, an uncanny instinct.

Whatever it is, Sereno had it that day. He laid his backpack on a rock and headed down into the little valley. He walked a dozen paces, straight to where a fossil was poking out of a sandstone ledge.

He was too experienced to get excited right away. The fossil most likely belonged to a rhynchosaur. The bones of those ancient owl-faced lizards had been popping out of the rock so often that the team had stopped collecting them.

Then Sereno looked more closely. A few neck bones had started to roll down the slope. Sereno rolled them back into place. And he realized that the neck bones led to the back of a skull. A *Herrerasaurus* skull.

For a few seconds he was frozen. Then he let out a huge yell that bounced off the distant cliffs and brought his teammates running.

As the others crowded around the skeleton to examine it more closely, Sereno walked away. He couldn't bear to look.

So much of what paleontologists do is pure grunt work. They spend their summers in dusty deserts, living on warm water, stale crackers, and tinned tuna, tripping over snakes and scorpions, going for weeks without a shower. Sereno was a talented but very young professor who was leading the first expedition of his life. People

thought he was crazy, that his chances of finding such a rare fossil in the middle of the desert were one in a million.

But, like Roy Chapman Andrews, he had set out to do it anyway.

Sereno walked back to the group and took another look. It was indeed a *Herrerasaurus* — the most complete skeleton that had ever been found.

He was so overwhelmed that he broke down and started to cry.

A though Paul Sereno knew that he had found a *Herrerasaurus*, he wanted to confirm that it was indeed the earliest dinosaur then known. He returned to the Valley of the Moon and, once again, luck was with him. Just a stone's throw from where he had found the *Herrerasaurus* skeleton, he uncovered a layer of greenish, popcornlike ash from an ancient volcano that had erupted at

Eoraptor or "Dawn Stealer"

In 1991, in the Valley of the Moon, Paul Sereno's team found a softball-sized piece of rock containing the tiny skull of *Eoraptor* (top). Further digging revealed a light-bodied, dog-sized dinosaur that ran on its hind legs (left). Like *Herrerasaurus*, *Eoraptor* is 228 million years old, but its body structure is more primitive, making it the oldest dinosaur yet discovered. *Eoraptor*'s back teeth were serrated like steak knives, but it did not have the mobile jaw joints of later carnivores.

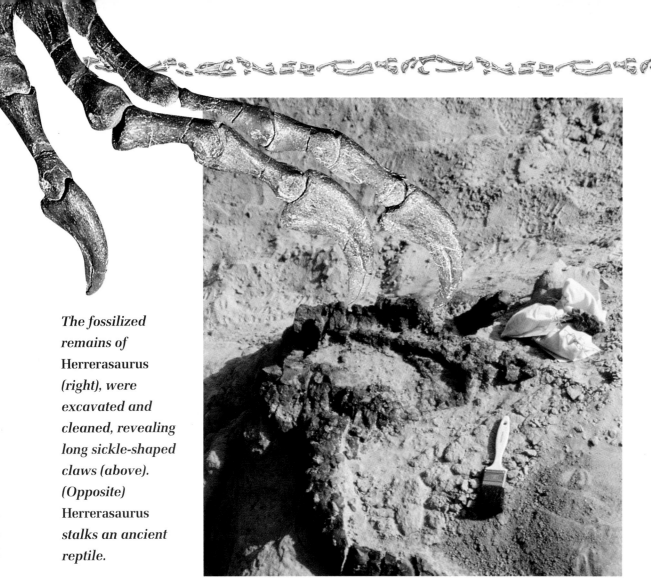

The fossilized remains of Herrerasaurus (right), were excavated and cleaned, revealing long sickle-shaped claws (above). (Opposite) Herrerasaurus stalks an ancient reptile.

including a grasshopperlike bug with wings a foot (thirty centimeters) long. But the river valley was also crawling with reptiles of all shapes and sizes. Some were furry, small, and fast. Some were fat ground crawlers with beaked and tusked heads. There were also lizards and crocodilelike meat-eaters such as *Saurosuchus* that preyed on dinosaurs.

Herrerasaurus was well equipped to compete in such a crowd.

It ran swiftly and gracefully on two legs, with its tail held out straight behind for balance. Being raised up on its hind legs improved its range of vision, and the complicated bone structure of its ears suggests it may have had excellent hearing. No doubt it was able to detect prey, and predators, on the noisy, crowded forest floor and wheel around quickly to flee or give chase.

the same time that *Herrerasaurus* died. The ash proved to be 228 million years old.

Paul Sereno's *Herrerasaurus* skeleton helped paleontologists move farther down the trunk of the dinosaurs' family tree. It showed that the first dinosaurs were probably meat-eaters, and that they were able to run quickly on two legs.

The earliest dinosaurs shared the earth with some very bizarre creatures. There were plenty of insects,

The skeleton that Paul Sereno found was smaller than other *Herrerasaurus* specimens that had been discovered. Only five feet (1.5 meters) long, it may have been a young one. But it had everything it needed to be an efficient hunter. Its big hands and sickle-shaped claws were perfectly designed for grabbing prey. Once the prey was in its mouth, *Herrerasaurus* would sink its big, finely serrated teeth into the flesh. An extra hinge in its lower

King of the Carnivores

Tyrannosaurus rex has long been considered the king of all carnivores. Scientists have done experiments to recreate the effect of its powerful jaws slamming 7-inch-long (18-cm) teeth into the bone of its prey and discovered that it could shut its mouth with the force of 3,000 pounds (1,364 kg) per square inch (2.5 cm), the same as an alligator. But two recent finds challenge *T. rex*'s role as king.

Giganotosaurus, discovered in Argentina in 1993, was slightly longer and heavier than *T. rex*. And in 1995, the huge skull (above) of *Carcharodontosaurus* or "shark-toothed reptile" was found by Paul Sereno in North Africa. The skull of this 90-million-year-old predator was slightly longer than that of the biggest *T. rex*, and its 5-inch-long (13-cm) teeth were ideal for slicing into the thick skin of plant-eaters. We don't know how long *Carcharodontosaurus* was since only its skull was found.

Even so some paleontologists believe that *T. rex*, being lighter and more advanced than both *Giganotosaurus* or *Carcharodontosaurus* would win in a fight against either of them.

Tyrannosaurus rex ▲
Length: 39 feet (11.7 m)
Skull length: 5 feet (1.5 m)
Weight: 6.4 tons

Giganotosaurus ▶
Length: 40 feet (12 m)
Skull length: 6 feet (1.8 m)
Weight: 9 tons

jaw allowed it to wrap its mouth around a creature that was too big to be swallowed whole, trapping it firmly until it stopped struggling.

Eventually, *Herrerasaurus*'s hunting and killing equipment were passed down to the huge carnivorous dinosaurs that terrorized the land millions of years later — with a few improvements. *Giganotosaurus* and *Tyrannosaurus rex*, both as long as a bus, were two of the biggest, meanest killers of them all. They used their powerful jaws and teeth to slice apart and crunch the bones of their prey.

And the sickle claw would reach deadly perfection in *Utahraptor*, whose fifteen-inch-long (thirty-eight-centimeter) killing claw could rip open the belly of a much larger enemy with a single kick.

Herrerasaurus handed down its gifts to an awesome range of creatures. Its descendants would rule the planet so successfully that it almost seemed as if they could last forever.

(Opposite) Carcharodontosaurus *snaps its massive jaws at a small but brave* Deltadromeus.

The forest floor was thick and damp, loud with the buzzing and cries of insects and animals. *Herrerasaurus* was on the hunt. It prowled along the side of the marsh, leaving a trail of three-toed footprints in the muddy ground. Its head darted from side to side, its ears and eyes trying to detect sound or movement that meant food.

A clap like thunder boomed in the distance, and the earth trembled. A small, furry creature darted along a tree branch. With a quick thrust of its head *Herrerasaurus* clamped its jaws on the animal and swallowed it whole.

But it was on the lookout for bigger prey. The toppled branches and thick ferns gave good cover to creatures of all kinds. The hunter had to be keen and quick.

A snap of a branch made its head turn. Its wary eyes caught the slight movement of a gray-green slab half-submerged in the marsh. The rhynchosaur was using its hind legs to dig roots and water plants out of the swamp.

It barely had time to raise its flat, beaky face before *Herrerasaurus* slashed at its neck with sharp claws. It clamped its jaws on the rhynchosaur, piercing the thick skin, and began to rip apart its flesh.

228 million years ago...
IN THE VOLCANO'S SHADOW
The Story of *Herrerasaurus*

A sound from behind made *Herrerasaurus* wheel suddenly, leaping to the side. The horny brow of a *Saurosuchus* split the surface of the water. It lumbered out of the swamp on all fours and heaved its body through the thick undergrowth, drawn by the smell of the fresh kill. It eyed the carcass and then *Herrerasaurus*.

Herrerasaurus raised itself tall on its hind legs and flashed its teeth. The *Saurosuchus* was twice its size, but *Herrerasaurus* was ready to defend its meal, and itself.

The ground trembled again, this time more violently. Water sloshed up over the edge of the marsh. From far beneath the earth came a deep, bellowing roar.

A giant crack split the air. Looking up, the creatures saw a huge tree slowly crashing toward them. *Herrerasaurus* leaped aside, but the slow-moving *Saurosuchus* was trapped, its body crushed by the massive trunk.

Winged creatures flew out of the forest in a spray. In the distance, the dark shape of a mountain seemed to split in two, and smoke and flames gushed from the summit. The sky grew dark and heavy, and a choking, sulfurous odor spread over the land. As *Herrerasaurus* shrieked in panic and confusion, gray ash began to fall, covering the dead, and the living, with a suffocating cloak.

Epilogue

Sandstorms, mass drownings, volcanoes. Many kinds of disasters killed off various groups of dinosaurs, but overall, the Age of Dinosaurs lasted for 165 million years. Their bones would one day be found on every continent, from the icy wastes of Antarctica to the hottest deserts of Africa and the wet jungles of Thailand.

How successful were they? Paleontologist Michael Novacek has explained the history of life on earth this way: Say that jellyfish and worms first appeared in the sea just over a week ago. Dinosaurs occupied the earth for two and a half days. And modern humans have been around for about the last ten minutes.

(Right) A giant asteroid may have crashed to earth, bringing an end to the Age of Dinosaurs.

Dinosaurs must have been exceptionally good at doing what they had to do to last so long. They adapted as needed to kill and find food, defend themselves against their enemies, as well as to produce and raise healthy young.

So what happened? Why are there no dinosaurs today? We have not found any fossils less than sixty-five million years old. What finally turned the entire planet into one big dinosaur graveyard?

Some scientists say it is because land masses shifted. Large bodies of water, including the huge inland sea that once split North America, dried up. Climates became more extreme, and many plants were unable to survive the change.

The plant-eating dinosaurs couldn't find enough to eat, so they died. Then the meat-eating dinosaurs had no plant-eaters to eat, so they died.

But many experts also think there must have been one single event that wiped out the dinosaurs and many other animals without killing off creatures such as birds, fishes, crocodiles, turtles, and small mammals. If a giant asteroid had smashed into the earth, for example, a huge dust cloud would have been created, blocking out the sun for several months. The darkness and cold would kill many plants. Smaller mammals and reptiles could have lived on insect larvae that fed on dead plants, but large creatures simply would not have been able to find enough to eat.

Scientists recently suggested that such an asteriod struck the Yucatán Peninsula of Mexico, leaving a crater more than 100 miles (160 km) across.

Or perhaps the truth lies in a combination of factors. Dinosaurs could already have been having a hard time. Perhaps they were having trouble surviving the changing climate. Along the Red Deer River of Alberta, for example, the number of species was already falling before the Age of

When did dinosaurs rule the earth?

More than three billion years ago, life on earth began with the first single cell. The first dinosaur did not appear until the middle of the Triassic period, between 248 and 213 million years ago. At that time the continents of the earth had joined forming a single supercontinent, Pangaea. Small meat-eating dinosaurs and early long-necked plant-eaters spread freely across the globe. But by the end of this period an ocean channel had separated Pangaea into two large land masses.

During the Jurassic period, 213 million to 144 million years ago, these land masses continued to break up. Giant long-necked plant-eaters were preyed on by large carnivorous dinosaurs, and plated dinosaurs appeared.

The continents drifted even further apart during the Cretaceous period, 144 million to 65 million years ago, although shallow seas allowed some animals to migrate between the continents. Dinosaurs, including duckbills, ankylosaurs, horned dinosaurs, and tyrannosaurs, flourished and then mysteriously died out. Since then, the continents have continued to drift apart, moving about one inch (2.5 cm) each year.

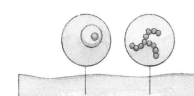

First single cell
3.5 billion years ago

Blue-green
algae

Wormlike organisms
with spinal chords

Jawless fish

Land plants

Amphibians

Reptiles

PALEOZOIC ERA
(570 – 290 million years ago)

Dinosaurs came to an end. Then, when there were few dinosaur species left, an asteriod hit the earth and finished them off. If it had hit earlier when the dinosaurs were stronger, they may have survived the impact.

Or maybe dinosaurs did not really become extinct at all. If they evolved into birds, as many paleontologists think, then they are still with us. As Mark Norell has said, birds are more closely related to *Tyrannosaurus rex* than *Tyrannosaurus rex* is to *Triceratops*. If you look at an ostrich or pileated woodpecker, it is not hard to see a family resemblance to the ancient beasts of the past.

But in the end, it is not the fact that dinosaurs are gone that interests so many people. What fascinates us about dinosaurs is the way they lived. They were peaceful browsers and vicious killers. They looked as weird as aliens and as familiar as garden lizards. They grew to almost impossible sizes, with killing claws and teeth more frightening than any horror movie has shown us. They thundered over the land, preyed on each other, ate monstrous amounts of vegetation, yet somehow left the earth intact for 165 million years. No wonder we think they may have something to teach us.

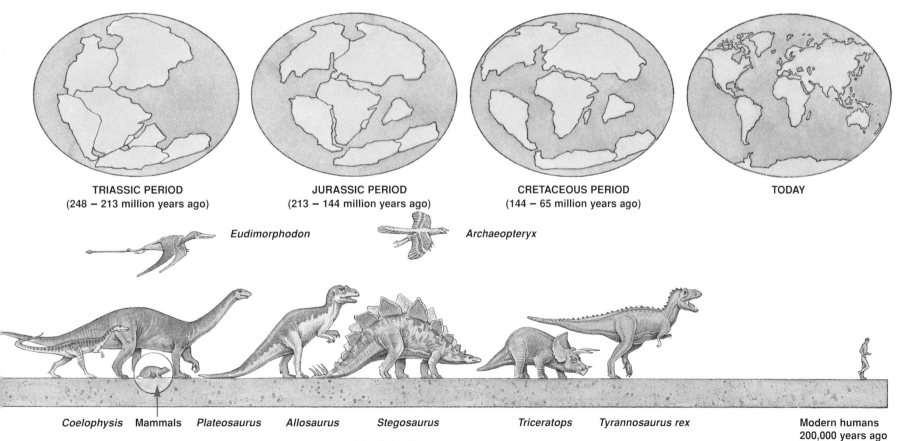

TRIASSIC PERIOD
(248 – 213 million years ago)

JURASSIC PERIOD
(213 – 144 million years ago)

CRETACEOUS PERIOD
(144 – 65 million years ago)

TODAY

Eudimorphodon

Archaeopteryx

Coelophysis Mammals *Plateosaurus* *Allosaurus* *Stegosaurus* *Triceratops* *Tyrannosaurus rex* Modern humans 200,000 years ago

MESOZOIC ERA
(248 – 65 million years ago)

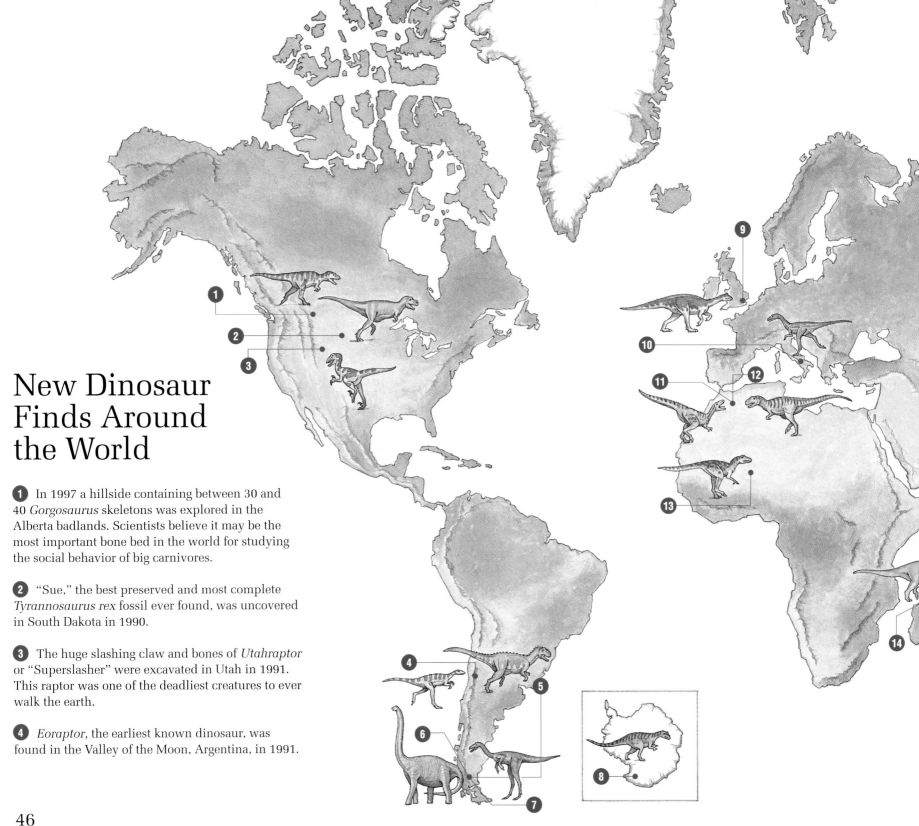

New Dinosaur Finds Around the World

1 In 1997 a hillside containing between 30 and 40 *Gorgosaurus* skeletons was explored in the Alberta badlands. Scientists believe it may be the most important bone bed in the world for studying the social behavior of big carnivores.

2 "Sue," the best preserved and most complete *Tyrannosaurus rex* fossil ever found, was uncovered in South Dakota in 1990.

3 The huge slashing claw and bones of *Utahraptor* or "Superslasher" were excavated in Utah in 1991. This raptor was one of the deadliest creatures to ever walk the earth.

4 *Eoraptor*, the earliest known dinosaur, was found in the Valley of the Moon, Argentina, in 1991.

5 *Giganotosaurus*, one of the biggest meat-eaters ever, was discovered in Argentina in 1993.

6 *Argentinosaurus*, one of the heaviest of the long-necked, plant-eating dinosaurs, was discovered in Patagonia, Argentina, in 1989.

7 *Unenlagia*, a meat-eating dinosaur with long arms that could be held in a winglike way, was identified in Patagonia, Argentina, in 1997.

8 *Cryolophosaurus* or "frozen-crested lizard," found in 1991, was the third dinosaur to be discovered on the Antarctic mainland.

9 Paleontologists have just completed a full scientific description of *Baryonyx*, a meat-eating dinosaur, found in Surrey, England, in 1983.

10 A young robin-sized dinosaur with big eyes was found in Italy in 1993. It is related to *Compsognathus*, but has not yet been given a name.

11 In 1995 the bones of a small but aggressive carnivore named *Deltadromeus*, the "delta runner," were discovered in the Sahara.

12 The huge skull of the deadly predator *Carcharodontosaurus* was uncovered in the Sahara in 1995.

13 The nearly complete skeleton of *Afrovenator*, or "African hunter," was unearthed in Niger in 1993. It was similar to *Allosaurus*, a predator that roamed North America long ago.

14 In Madagascar, in 1996, a beautifully preserved *Majungotholus* skull was found, proving that this dinosaur was a new kind of meat-eater, not a pachycephalosaur as had previously been thought.

15 An *Oviraptor* was discovered sitting on a nest of its own eggs in the Gobi Desert in 1993.

16 An amazing treasure trove of dinosaur fossils was found in Northeast China, in 1996, including *Sinosauropteryx*, a small birdlike dinosaur that may have had an early form of feathers covering its body.

17 A new raptor with a huge sickle claw was excavated in Japan, in 1993, at a site rich in dinosaur fossils.

18 The fossil bones of the oldest known tyrannosaur, *Siamotyrannus*, were found in a jungle stream in Thailand in 1993. This find supports the idea that tyrannosaurs developed in Asia and spread over a land bridge to North America.

19 The scientific study of *Minmi*, a new ankylosaur discovered in Queensland, Australia, in 1989, has just been completed.

47

Glossary

ankylosaur: One of the family of heavily armored, four-footed, plant-eating dinosaurs that lived during the Cretaceous period.

asteroid: A small rocky body that revolves around the sun.

carnivore: An animal, often with powerful jaws and teeth, that feeds on animal flesh.

carrion: Dead, rotting flesh.

duckbill: A large plant-eating dinosaur, with a snout shaped like a duck's bill, that lived during the late Cretaceous period. Duckbills are also called hadrosaurs.

evolution: The gradual development from simple to more complex forms of life.

excavation: The process of digging out and removing an object from the ground.

fossil: The remains or impression of a prehistoric animal or plant that has turned to stone.

herbivore: An animal that eats plants.

pachycephalosaur: One of the family of dinosaurs with very thick skull bones that lived during the Cretaceous period.

paleontologist: A scientist who studies the fossils of animals and plants.

pterosaur: Any of a group of extinct flying reptiles that lived from the late Triassic period to the Cretaceous period.

rhynchosaur: One of the family of plant-eating lizards that first appeared on earth in the middle of the Triassic period.

sedimentary rock: Rock that is formed by deposits of sediment — soil and sand carried by water, wind, or glaciers.

serrated: Having an edge like that on the blade of a saw or steak knife.

sickle-shaped claw: A claw that is curved in the shape of a sickle blade. A sickle is a short-handled farming tool with a semi-circular blade.

skeletal: Relating to a skeleton.

tyrannosaur: One of the family of large, two-footed, meat-eating dinosaurs with powerful jaws and hind legs, small claw-like front legs, and a large tail, that lived during the late Cretaceous period.

Recommended Further Reading

Digging Up Tyrannosaurus Rex
by John R. Horner and Don Lessem
(*Crown Publishers, Inc.*)

Paleontologist Jack Horner describes the excavation of one of the most complete *Tyrannosaurus rex* fossils ever found.

Dinosaur Worlds
by Don Lessem
(*Boyds Mills Press*)

A comprehensive, fully illustrated look at dinosaurs and other prehistoric creatures in their natural habitats, including the latest findings about "new" dinosaurs.

Make Your Own Dinosaur Out of Chicken Bones
by Chris McGowan
(*HarperCollins Publishers Inc.*)

This fascinating guide for budding paleontologists explains how to make dinosaur skeletons out of chicken bones in your own kitchen.

Picture Credits

All illustrations are by Alan Barnard unless otherwise stated.

Front cover: Illustration © Mark Hallett. (Top left) Paul Sereno unearths *Carcharodontosaurus* and (top right) a *Herrerasaurus* skull, both courtesy of Paul Sereno. (Bottom left) C. Wallis. (Bottom right) Gordon Reid.

Back cover: (Top right and bottom) Louis Psihoyos, Matrix International, Inc.

Endpapers: C. Wallis.

1: Louis Psihoyos, Matrix International, Inc.

4: (Middle inset) Gordon Reid. (Right inset) Paul Sereno.

4–5: Louis Psihoyos, Matrix International, Inc.

6: Michael Skrepnick.

6–7: #17244 (Photo by Mark Norell) Courtesy Dept. of Library Services, American Museum of Natural History.

8: Design motif by Jack McMaster. (Top) neg.#410783 (Photo by J. B. Shackelford) and (Inset) neg.#K17175, both courtesy Dept. of Library Services, American Museum of Natural History.

9: (Top left) neg.#5412(2), (Top right) neg.#K17241 and (Middle right) neg.#312325, photo by Julius Kirschner; all courtesy Dept. of Library Services, American Museum of Natural History. (Bottom) Louis Psihoyos, Matrix International, Inc.

10: (Top) Louis Psihoyos, Matrix International, Inc. (Inset) Photo by Amy Davidson, American Museum of Natural History.

11: Map by Jack McMaster. (Bottom left) Cover illustration by Thomas W. Voter. (Bottom right) neg. #411309 (Photo by J. B. Shackelford) Courtesy Dept. of Library Services, American Museum of Natural History.

12: Louis Psihoyos, Matrix International, Inc.

13: Diagram by Jack McMaster.

14: (Top) #5789 (Photo by Denis Finnin) Courtesy Dept. of Library Services, American Museum of Natural History. (Middle left) Louis Psihoyos, Matrix International, Inc. (Bottom left) neg.#K17089 (Drawing by Michael Ellison) Courtesy Dept. of Library Services, American Museum of Natural History. (Bottom right) Donna Sloan, Royal Tyrrell Museum of Palaeontology.

16: Illustration © Mark Hallett. (Inset) Louis Psihoyos, Matrix International, Inc.

17: (Top) The Natural History Museum, London. Diagram by Jack McMaster.

18–19: Illustration © John Sibbick.

19: Bruce Selyem, Museum of the Rockies.

22: C. Wallis.

23: (Inset) Gordon Reid. Maps by Jack McMaster.

24: (Left) Louis Psihoyos, Matrix International, Inc. (Top) Illustration © Michael Skrepnick. (Bottom) Gordon Reid.

25: Diagram by Jack McMaster.

26: Royal Tyrrell Museum/Alberta Community Development.

27: Illustration © Michael Skrepnick.

28: Philip J. Currie.

32: Louis Psihoyos, Matrix International, Inc.

33: (Top) Louis Psihoyos, Matrix International, Inc. Map by Jack McMaster.

34: Louis Psihoyos, Matrix International, Inc.

35: (Top) Louis Psihoyos, Matrix International, Inc. (Bottom) Illustration © John Sibbick.

36: Paul Sereno.

38: (Top) Paul Sereno.

39: Illustration © Mark Hallett.

44–45: Diagram by Jack McMaster.

46–47: Map and diagrams by Jack McMaster.

Acknowledgments

Madison Press Books would like to thank the following individuals for their invaluable assistance: our principal consultant, Philip J. Currie of the Royal Tyrrell Museum of Palaeontology, as well as consultants Mark Norell and Paul Sereno; Gordon Reid; Donna Sloan; and Paula Willey, Special Collections, the American Museum of Natural History.